SOCCER SUPERSTARS

MBAPPÉ
RULES

WELBECK

Hi, pleased to meet you.

We hope you enjoy our book about Kylian Mbappé!

SIMON   DAN

THIS IS A WELBECK CHILDREN'S BOOK
Published in the USA in 2020 by Welbeck Children's Books
Limited
An imprint of the Welbeck Publishing Group
20 Mortimer Street, London W1T 3JW
Text, design and illustration © Welbeck Publishing Limited 2020
ISBN: 978-1-78312-584-5

Writer: Simon Mugford
Designer and Illustrator: Dan Green
Design manager: Emily Clarke
Executive editor: Suhel Ahmed
Production: Nicola Davey

Printed in the UK
10 9 8 7 6 5 4 3 2 1

Statistics and records correct as of January 2020

SOCCER SUPERSTARS

MBAPPÉ

RULES

SIMON MUGFORD   DAN GREEN

CONTENTS

CHAPTER 1

MBAPPÉ MMAZING

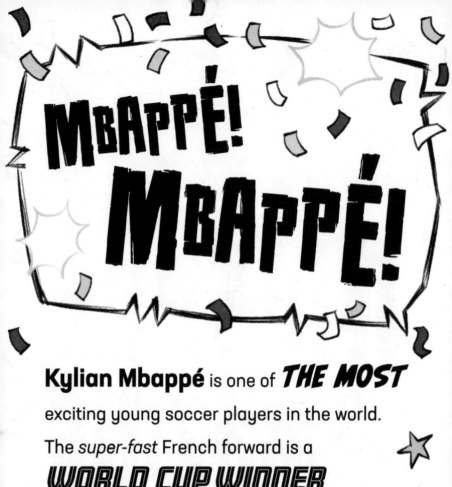

MBAPPÉ! MBAPPÉ!

Kylian Mbappé is one of ***THE MOST***

exciting young soccer players in the world.

The *super-fast* French forward is a

WORLD CUP WINNER

and an

AMAZING

STRIKER.

WHAT MAKES **MBAPPÉ** SO FANTASTIC?

Let's find out!

Speed
One of the fastest players in the world.

Dribbling
Awesome at getting past defenders with the ball at his feet.

Tricks
Master of the fancy flick and super stepovers.

Timing
Knows exactly when to make dangerous runs at his opponents.

LET'S LOOK AT THE NUMBERS TO SEE WHY MBAPPÉ RULES.

3 ...3 Ligue 1 titles

1 ...French Cup win

1 ...French League Cup win

81 ...goals for Paris Saint-Germain

1 . . . **World Cup** win

13 . . . goals for France

Estimated
$200 MILLION transfer fee

37 MILLION
followers on Instagram

MBAPPÉ I.D.

NAME:
Kylian Mbappé Lottin

NICKNAME: *37*

DATE OF BIRTH:
December 20, 1998

PLACE OF BIRTH:
Paris, France

HEIGHT: *5'10" (1.78 m)*

POSITION: *Forward*

CLUBS: *Monaco,*
Paris Saint-Germain (PSG)

NATIONAL TEAM: *France*

LEFT OR RIGHT-FOOTED: *Right*

1998 was a **BIG year** for **French** soccer. In July, France beat **Brazil** in **Paris** to win the **World Cup** for the first time.

Then in December, in the Paris suburb of **Bondy,** Kylian Mbappé was born.

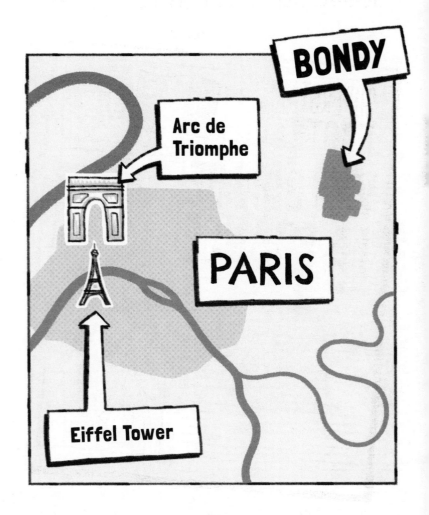

Bondy is not like the **rich, famous** parts of ***PARIS*** with tourists, art galleries, and museums.

16

MEET KYLIAN'S SPORTS-CRAZY FAMILY

Wilfried

His dad was a player and coach at the local team, AS Bondy.

Fayza

His mom played handball in the French first division.

Ethan

Kylian's younger brother is a youth player at PSG.

Jirès Kembo Okoko

His adopted brother is a professional soccer player, too!

 Why was the soccer player upset on their birthday?

 Because they got a red card!

Kylian **LOVED** soccer from the
first time he kicked a ball.
When his dad played and coached at
AS Bondy, little Kylian was there,
listening to the team talks.

23

When he was six, Kylian plays for Bondy's under-7s. Dribbling, passing, scoring –**Kylian was great at them all.** He was the **_BEST PLAYER_** by far.

BoFF!

THE COACHES COULD NOT BELIEVE HOW GOOD HE WAS.

Kylian played in the under-11s when he was eight.

Kylian idolized players like **Thierry Henry** and **Lionel Messi**, but his favorite player was . . .

Kylian wanted to be just like him, so he practiced Ronaldo's **TRICKS, RUNS,** and **GOALS!**

Kylian was 13 when he won a place at the famous French soccer academy **Clairefontaine.** Players like **Nicolas Anelka, Olivier Giroud,** and one of Kylian's heroes, **Thierry Henry,** had all trained there.

WOW, this place is really fancy!

Kylian trained on the amazing fields at **Clairefontaine** during the week, but on weekends, he went home to play with his friends at **Bondy!**

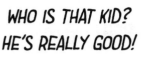

WHO IS THAT KID? HE'S REALLY GOOD!

Kylian started to get his own **fans**. **Managers** from some **big clubs** came to see him play!

Some of the **BIGGEST** *CLUBS* in
Europe wanted to sign Kylian.

He even tried out for
Chelsea, but said,

NO THANKS!

He even said **no thanks** to **REAL MADRID**,
where he might have played with his hero

RONALDO!

"HE CAN BECOME AS GREAT AS **PELÉ, MARADONA,** AND **MESSI.**"

Former PSG teammate and legendary Italian goalkeeper Gianluigi Buffon

CHAPTER 4

MONACO MARVEL

Kylian did not want to live too far from his **family,** so he joined **Monaco** in **JULY 2013.**

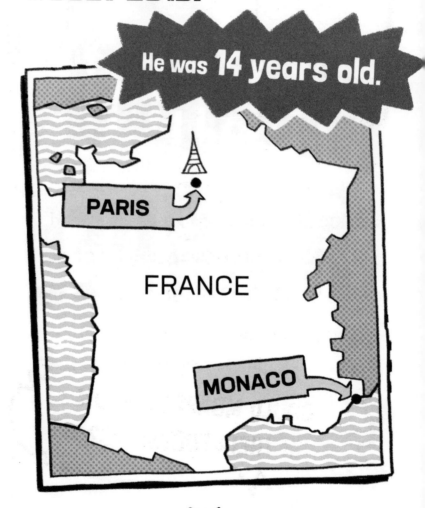

He was **14 years old.**

PARIS

FRANCE

MONACO

Monaco had a great history. French World Cup-winners like **Emmanuel Petit** and Kylian's hero **Thierry Henry** went through its youth academy.

COULD MBAPPÉ FOLLOW IN THEIR FOOTSTEPS?

Kylian made his **Ligue 1 debut** for Monaco, at home to **CAEN** in December 2015. Liverpool's **Fabinho** and Manchester City's **Bernardo Silva** were on the same team.

Kylian scored his **first goal** for Monaco two months later—a **93rd-minute** shot against **Troyes.**

GOoOOOO

MBAPPÉ VERSUS HENRY

MBAPPÉ

AGE AT DEBUT: **16 years, 347 days**

AGE DEBUT GOAL SCORED: **17 years 62 days**

APPEARANCES: **60**

GOALS: **27**

How does **Mbappé** compare to Monaco's previous teenage sensation, French icon **Thierry Henry?**

HENRY

AGE AT DEBUT: **17 years, 15 days**

AGE DEBUT GOAL SCORED: **17 years 224 days**

APPEARANCES: **139**

GOALS: **28**

MONACO HIGHLIGHTS

SOME OF THE BIGGEST GAMES OF MBAPPÉ'S MONACO CAREER.

DECEMBER 14, 2016

COUPE DE LA LIGUE, ROUND OF 16

Monaco 7-0 Rennes

Mbappé scored his first Monaco hat trick in this decisive victory over Rennes.

FEBRUARY 11, 2017

LIGUE 1

Monaco 5-0 FC Metz

Another hat trick! Mbappé went on to score another eight goals in his next four league games.

APRIL 19, 2017

CHAMPIONS LEAGUE QUARTERFINAL, SECOND LEG

Monaco 3-1 Borussia Dortmund (6-3 agg)

Kylian's goal in this match was his fifth Champions League goal of the season!

MAN CITY MOMENT

MARCH 15, 2017

CHAMPIONS LEAGUE LAST 16, SECOND LEG

Monaco 3-1 Manchester City (6-6 agg)

44

Kylian scored his **first Champions League goal** in the first leg, but **MONACO** lost **5-3.** It would take a lot of goals to catch up!

In the eighth minute, Bernardo Silva crossed the ball and . . . **BOINK!** Kylian was there to nutmeg the keeper.

GOAAALLLL!

Monaco went through on the away-goals rule!

2016-17 was **Mbappé's** first

full season for **Monaco.**

ALL-COMPETITIONS RECORD

APPEARANCES	ASSISTS	GOALS
44	14	26

KYLIAN'S GOALS HELPED
MONACO BECOME LIGUE 1
CHAMPIONS FOR
THE FIRST TIME
IN 17 YEARS.

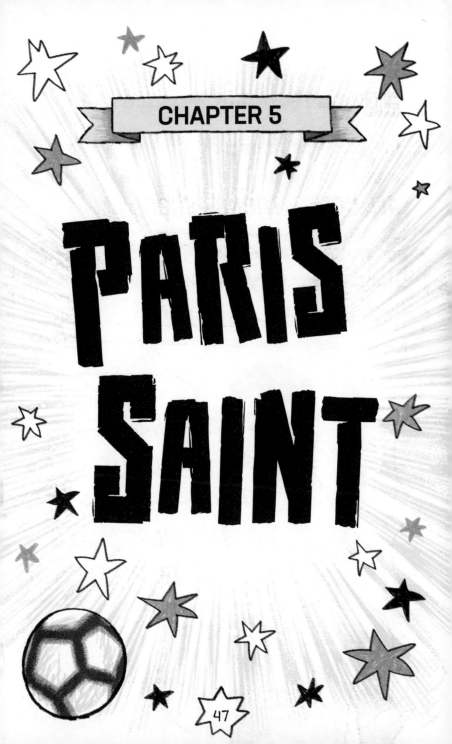

CHAPTER 5

PARIS SAINT

Kylian's record at Monaco had made him **a star.** Europe's biggest clubs wanted to sign him.

This time, he said "NO THANKS!" to **Manchester City,** and "NO THANKS!" to **Real Madrid** – *AGAIN!*

He was a **Paris boy**—so it was

PARIS SAINT-GERMAIN

FOR KYLIAN!

He went on loan to them in **August 2017**.

REAL MADRID HAD:

Karim **B**enzema, Gareth **B**ale, and **C**ristiano Ronaldo:

BBC

Karim Benzema

Gareth Bale

Cristiano Ronaldo

BARCELONA USED TO HAVE:

Lionel **M**essi, Luis **S**uárez, and **N**eymar:

Lionel Messi

Luis Suárez

MSN

Neymar

PSG HAD ALREADY BOUGHT NEYMAR FROM BARCELONA SO NOW HAD:

Kylian **M**bappé, Edinson **C**avani, and **N**eymar:

MCN

Kylian Mbappé

Edinson Cavani

Neymar

PSG HAD A PLAN TO BECOME THE BIGGEST CLUB IN EUROPE.

The most expensive player in the world!

FIRST GAME, FIRST GOAL

SEPTEMBER 8, 2017

FC Metz 1-5 PSG

It was **Kylian's first game** for PSG. In the **59th minute,** a Metz defender cleared the ball straight to Kylian . . .

BOOM!

He **FIRED** it straight into the net.

GOAAALLL!

This was the first game where "MCN" each scored a goal!

2017-18 HIGHLIGHTS

THE BEST OF MBAPPÉ'S FIRST SEASON AT PSG

SEPTEMBER 12, 2017

CHAMPIONS LEAGUE GROUP STAGE

Celtic 0-5 PSG

Kylian's first European goal for PSG came in this Champions League thrashing of Celtic.

DECEMBER 5, 2017

CHAMPIONS LEAGUE GROUP STAGE

Bayern Munich 3-1 PSG

Kylian was on the losing side, but he scored his TENTH Champions League goal.

Kylian became the youngest player to score ten Champions League goals!

APRIL 18, 2018

COUPE DE FRANCE SEMIFINAL

Caen 1-3 PSG

Two goals from Kylian helped his team reach the French Cup final, and a PSG win!

The more **goals** he scored, the more times Kylian could perform his **favorite goal celebration.**

Kylian **borrowed this celebration** from his brother **Ethan.** He did it whenever he scored a goal—*PLAYING FIFA!*

PSG TROPHY #1

MARCH 31, 2018

COUPE DE LA LIGUE FINAL

STADE DE BORDEAUX

PSG 3-0 Monaco

Kylian won his first trophy with **PSG**

—THE FRENCH LEAGUE CUP—

against his old club!

He didn't score a goal, but had **two assists** and won a **penalty.**

KYLIAN WAS "MAN OF THE MATCH"!

TREBLE TIME

Paris Saint-Germain won **Ligue 1** with **five** games to go when they beat **MONACO 7-1!** They finished **13 points** ahead of Monaco.

LIGUE 1 TROPHY

Kylian and his teammates ended the season by beating **LES HERBIERS 2-0** in the **COUPE DE FRANCE** final.

He had won an incredible **THREE** trophies in his first season!

COUPE DE FRANCE

COUPE DE LA LIGUE

2017-18

It was an **AWESOME** first season for **Kylian** at **PSG.**

APPEARANCES	ASSISTS	GOALS
44	21	15

He was voted *Ligue 1 Young Player of the Year!*

CHAPTER 6

TEENAGE ICON

When **Mbappé** signed for

PARIS SAINT-GERMAIN

the fee was an estimated

$200 MILLION.

Kylian was the **MOST EXPENSIVE TEENAGE SOCCER PLAYER** in the world.

In 2018, Kylian appeared on the cover of **TIME** magazine. He was described as "the future of soccer."

Lionel Messi, Neymar, and Mario Balotelli are the only other players to appear on a **TIME** cover.

CHAPTER 7

WORLD CLASS

In 2016, Kylian played for **France** at his first international tournament–the **European Under–19 Championship.**

He scored against **Croatia** and the **Netherlands** before getting **two goals** and an assist to beat **Portugal** in the semifinal.

France went on to beat **Italy 4–0**

in the final, which made Kylian a

EUROPEAN CHAMPION!

In 2017, France played in a **WORLD CUP** qualifying match. The finals would be held in Russia the following year. **18-year-old** Kylian was called into the senior squad.

WHAT AN HONOR!

His debut was against **Luxembourg,** and he scored his first goal against the **Netherlands.**

France won the group and was headed to

THE WORLD CUP!

WORLD CUP 2018

JUNE 21, 2018

WORLD CUP GROUP C

France 1-0 Peru

France faced **Peru** in its **second match** of the tournament. In the **34th minute,** Kylian picked up a deflected shot from

Olivier Giroud and

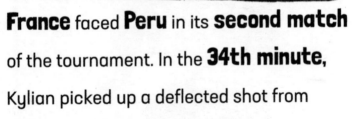

BOINK

—he had the ball in the back of the goal!

KYLIAN CELEBRATED WITH HIS FAVORITE CELEBRATION!

Mbappé is the youngest-ever French scorer at a World Cup.

He was 19 years, 183 days old!

France was up against **Lionel Messi's Argentina** in the **knockout round.** Kylian won a penalty that **Antoine Griezmann** scored . . . but shortly after halftime, France was **losing 2–1!**

78

Benjamin Pavard scored to tie it up **2-2**, and then it was Kylian's turn. He scored not one, but **TWO** awesome goals!

HIS TEAMMATES WENT WILD.

LIONEL MESSI

Argentina pulled one back, but France went through and Kylian was

WORLD FAMOUS!

MBAPPÉ RULES!

WORLD CUP FINAL

JULY 15, 2018

WORLD CUP FINAL

France 4-2 Croatia

The final was a crazy match! There was a **THUNDERSTORM,** a dodgy **PENALTY,** an **OWN GOAL,** a **GOALKEEPING MISTAKE,** but importantly

for Kylian, he scored

a goal in the

WORLD CUP FINAL!

FRANCE WON the tournament for the first time since **1998** –the year Kylian was born. Now, **at just 19,** he was a

WORLD CHAMPION!

MBAPPÉ VERSUS PELÉ

Kylian scored **FOUR** goals and won the **World Cup Best Young Player Award** at the **2018 World Cup.** He has been compared to **PELÉ**–perhaps the best player of all time.

Kylian was the youngest French player to score at a **World Cup** and the youngest scorer in a final since **Pelé in 1958.**

"WHAT HE CAN DO AT SUCH A YOUNG AGE IS NOT NORMAL . . . THERE ARE A LOT OF KYLIANS, BUT ONLY ONE KYLIAN MBAPPÉ."

France manager Didier Deschamps

84

TOP BOY

At the start of the 2018-19

season for PSG, Kylian was given

a new number.

He was going to wear **NUMBER 7**–just like his hero, **Cristiano Ronaldo.**

Kylian scored **TWICE** in his first game of the season—a **3-1** win over **Guingamp** in Ligue 1.

Then in the next game, **Mbappé,** **Cavani,** and **Neymar,** each scored a goal in a **3=1** win over **Angers.**

LIGUE 1 2018–19 HIGHLIGHTS

OCTOBER 7, 2018
PSG 5-0 Lyon

*Kylian won a penalty, which Neymar scored, then went on to score **FOUR** goals!*

JANUARY 19, 2019
PSG 9-0 Guingamp

*Kylian and Cavani both scored **hat tricks**, and Neymar netted two goals in this demolition!*

APRIL 21, 2019
PSG 3-1 Monaco

*Kylian's third hat trick of the season (against his old club **Monaco**!) helped PSG become league champions.*

WONDER GOAL

SEPTEMBER 1, 2018

Nimes 2-4 PSG

Kylian scored one of his **best goals** of the season when he picked up a long ball from **Presnel Kimpembe** and–

BOooooM

–he smashed it into the back of the net!

TOP SCORER

Kylian was the **top scorer** in **Ligue 1** that season, with ***33 GOALS.*** Across Europe, only **Lionel Messi** had a better league goal record that season!

Mbappé was the

LIGUE 1 PLAYER OF THE YEAR

and

YOUNG PLAYER OF THE YEAR 2018-19.

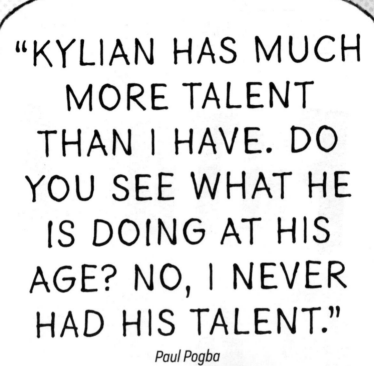

96

100 GOALS

In June 2019, Kylian scored for **France** in a **EURO 2020** qualifying game against **Andorra.**

BOFF!

IT WAS HIS **100TH** PROFESSIONAL GOAL!

GOAL!

He was 20 years, 5 months old.

WHO WAS THE FASTEST TO 100 GOALS?

NEYMAR
20 YEARS, 1 MONTH
173 GAMES

MBAPPÉ
20 YEARS, 5 MONTHS
180 GAMES

MESSI

22 YEARS, 3 MONTHS

214 GAMES

RONALDO

22 YEARS, 11 MONTHS

298 GAMES

*I SCORED **100** GOALS FASTER!*

SID CENTIPEDE
STRIKER FOR
CRAWLEY TOWN FC

MBAPPÉ VS NEYMAR VS MESSI VS RONALDO

WHO'S BEST FOR THEIR CLUB IN ALL COMPETITIONS?

2016-17	GAMES	GOALS	ASSISTS
MBAPPÉ	44	26	11
NEYMAR	45	20	26
RONALDO	46	42	11
MESSI	52	54	16

2017-18	GAMES	GOALS	ASSISTS
MBAPPÉ	46	21	18
NEYMAR	30	28	16
RONALDO	44	44	8
MESSI	54	45	18

2018-19	GAMES	GOALS	ASSISTS
MBAPPÉ	43	39	17
NEYMAR	28	23	13
RONALDO	43	28	10
MESSI	50	51	22

FRANCE'S FINEST

Kylian has a ways to go before before he catches up with the great French players.

But **winning the World Cup** at **19** is a **good start!**

KYLIAN MBAPPÉ
2017–

 33
CAPS

 13
GOALS

 **1**
WORLD CUP

THIERRY HENRY *1997-2010*

123
CAPS

51
GOALS

1
WORLD CUP

1
EUROPEAN
CHAMPIONSHIP

MICHEL PLATINI
1976-1987

72
CAPS

41
GOALS

1
EUROPEAN
CHAMPIONSHIP

OLIVIER GIROUD
2011-

97
CAPS

39
GOALS

1
WORLD CUP

"WHEN KYLIAN DOES WHAT CRISTIANO DID IN MADRID – THINKING ONLY ABOUT SCORING – THEN HE WILL DO THE SAME. HE WILL BE SCORING 50 GOALS PER SEASON."

Antoine Griezmann

HAT-TRICK HERO

OCTOBER 22, 2019

CHAMPIONS LEAGUE GROUP STAGE

Club Brugge 0-5 PSG

Kylian had been out with an **injury** and started on the **bench.** He came on in the **52nd minute** and . . .

scored with his **head . . .**

assisted **Mauro Icardi** for a goal . . .

scored with his

right foot . . .

then scored with

his **left foot!**

In just over **20 minutes**

he had scored his

first *CHAMPIONS*

LEAGUE HAT TRICK!

CHAMPIONS LEAGUE GOALS SCORED AT THE AGE OF 20:

Kylian is the youngest player to score 15 Champions League goals.

 KYLIAN MBAPPÉ *19 goals*

 KARIM BENZEMA *12 goals*

	**PATRICK KLUIVERT**	*9 goals*
	RAÚL	*8 goals*
	OBAFEMI MARTINS	*8 goals*
	**LIONEL MESSI**	*8 goals*
	**JAVIER SAVIOLA**	*8 goals*
	**THIERRY HENRY**	*7 goals*

PARIS GREATS

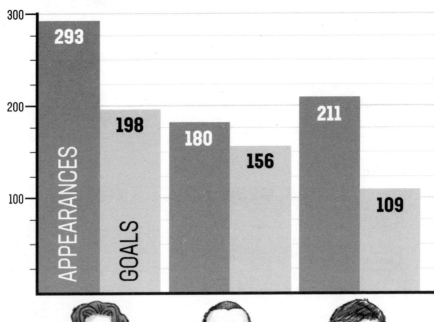

293

198

180

156

211

109

APPEARANCES

GOALS

EDINSON CAVANI

ZLATAN IBRAHIMOVIĆ

PAULETA

112

THESE ARE SOME OF PARIS SAINT-GERMAIN'S TOP SCORERS. HOW FAR WILL KYLIAN GO?

206

79

109

81

KYLIAN MBAPPÉ

ÁNGEL DI MARIA

The **REAL MADRID** manager **Zinedine Zidane** thinks Kylian is

AWESOME.

> **HE'D PROBABLY LIKE TO SIGN HIM FOR HIS TEAM!**

In November 2019, he said:

"I'VE BEEN IN LOVE WITH HIM FOR A LONG, LONG TIME ..."

Kylian got a bonus for the **World Cup win**, and donated it **ALL** to **charity**.

He gives the money he earns for each **France** game to charities, too.

THANKS, KYLIAN!

Mbappé is one of the **FASTEST** players in soccer. He was recorded running at **23.6 mph** in a game against **Monaco** in April 2019.

That's very fast! But not quite as fast as **USAIN BOLT,** the fastest man on the planet. His top speed was **27 mph.**

Usain Bolt wanted to be a soccer player!

Usain Bolt

STEPOVER STAR

Kylian learned **tricks** like the step over by copying his **hero, Ronaldo.** His opponent thinks he's going *one way* . . . but then he goes **another way!**

1

HE RUNS HARD, THEN SWINGS ONE FOOT AROUND THE BALL.

THEN SWINGS THE OTHER FOOT THE SAME WAY VERY FAST!

AND GETS PAST THE DEFENDER — SEE YOU LATER!

TROPHY CABINET

Kylian has **won a lot** for such a **young player**.

LIGUE 1 WINNER
2016-17 (MONACO)
2017-18 (PSG)
2018-19 (PSG)

LIGUE 1 TOP SCORER
2018-19

COUPE DE FRANCE WINNER
2017-18

COUPE DE LA LIGUE WINNER
2017-18

TROPHÉE DES CHAMPIONS WINNER
2019

WORLD CUP WINNER
2018

QUIZ TIME!

How much do you know about Mbappé? Try this quiz to find out, then test your friends!

1. Which local team did Kylian play for in his hometown?

----

2. How many goals did Kylian score for Monaco in 2016-17?

----

3. Which magazine described Mbappé as "The Future of Football"?

----

4. Against which team did Kylian score his first European goal for PSG?

----

5. What does MCN stand for?

----

6. In which season did Mbappé win the domestic treble with PSG?

----

7. How many goals did Kylian score against Argentina in the 2018 World Cup?

----

8. Mbappé is the second-youngest player to score in a World Cup final. Who is the youngest?

----

9. Which uniform number did Kylian take at PSG in 2018-19?

----

10. How many Champions League goals had Mbappé scored by the age of 20?

The answers are on the next page . . . *but no peeking!*

ANSWERS

1. AS Bondy
2. 26
3. *Time*
4. Celtic
5. Mbappé Cavani Neymar
6. 2017–18
7. Two
8. Pelé
9. 7
10. 19

MBAPPÉ:
WORDS YOU NEED TO KNOW

Coupe de France
The top knockout cup competition in France.

Coupe de la Ligue
The second knockout competition in France. The French League Cup.

Golden Boy
Award for the best player in Europe under 21.

Ligue 1
The top soccer league in France.

Trophée des Champions
Trophy awarded to the winner of a match between the Ligue 1 champions and the Coupe de France winners.

UEFA Champions League
European club competition held every year. The winner is the best team in Europe.

ABOUT THE AUTHORS

Simon's first job was at the Science Museum in London, making paper airplanes and blowing bubbles big enough for your dad to stand in. Since then he's written all sorts of books about the stuff he likes, from dinosaurs and rockets, to llamas, loud music, and of course, soccer. Simon has supported Ipswich Town since they won the FA Cup in 1978 (it's true—look it up) and once sat next to Rio Ferdinand on a train. He lives in Kent, England with his wife and daughter, two tortoises, and a cat.

Dan has drawn silly pictures since he could hold a crayon. Then he grew up and started making books about stuff like trucks, space, people's jobs, *Doctor Who,* and *Star Wars.* Dan remembers Ipswich Town winning the FA Cup but he didn't watch it because he was too busy making a Viking ship out of brown paper. As a result, he knows more about Vikings than soccer. Dan lives in Suffolk, England with his wife, son, daughter, and a dog that takes him for very long walks.